CAGELOVE

Christopher Denham

I0139895

BROADWAY PLAY PUBLISHING INC
New York
www.broadwayplaypublishing.com
info@broadwayplaypublishing.com

CAGELOVE
© Copyright 2007 Christopher Denham

Cover image by Bevin O'Gara
1st printing: February 2007
I S B N: 978-0-88145-329-4

Book design: Marie Donovan
Word processing: Microsoft Word
Typographic controls: Ventura Publisher
Typeface: Palatino
Printed and bound in the U S A

CAGELOVE was first presented in New York City on 10 May 2006 by Rattlestick Playwright's Theater (David Van Asselt, Artistic Director). The cast was as follows:

SAM ....Daniel Eric Gold
KATIE .... Gillian Jacobs
ELLEN .... Emily Cass McDonnell

Director ....Adam Rapp
Set design .... John McDermott
Lighting design .... Ed McCarthy
Sound design .... Eric Shim
Costume design .... Erika Monro
Production stage manager ....Paige Van den Burg

CAGELOVE was made possible by a generous donation from the Ovid Fund For New Plays, Jon Robin Baitz, Director.

CHARACTERS & SETTING

KATIE CORBIN, *twenty-five. Stunning. A photographer.*

SAM ROSENSTEIN, *twenty-seven.* KATIE's *fiancé.*
A computer programmer.

ELLEN CORBIN, *thirty.* KATIE's *sister. Psychology student.*

Time: A week in April.

Place: A Chicago apartment.

The author wishes to thank: David Van Asselt, the bravest producer in New York; Anthony Rapp, whose direction made my play a better play; Andy Gershenzon, Abbey Siegworth, Holley Fain, Danny Goldstein, and Justin Waldman for their particpation in previous productions. And special thanks to Daniel Sullivan for getting me out of central Illinois.

Scene One

(An apartment in Chicago. The Lincoln Park neighborhood)

(A futon type thing. A window with bars. A small table with two chairs. A hallway to a kitchen. A closet.)

(SAM [twenty-seven] enters, flips on the lights and sets down a bag. He leaves, reenters holding KATIE, a stunning twenty-five year old, whom he helps to the bed.)

(Then, a long, long pause)

(KATIE stands, walks into the kitchen.)

(SAM takes off his coat. Hangs it up. Takes a small bag of pills from KATIE's bag. Places the three pill bottles on the night stand.)

(KATIE comes back with a can of spaghetti-Os. Pause)

KATIE: *(Singing softly)* Uh-oh Spaghetti Os. Uh-oh Spaghetti Os. Watch your toes, uh-oh Spaghetti Os.

(KATIE kisses SAM.)

KATIE: Wipe your nose—Uh-oh Spaghetti-Os. *(She takes a bite.)* This stuff blows—Uh-oh spaghetti-Os.

(KATIE offers some to SAM, who refuses. KATIE then eats the entire can in silence.)

KATIE: What?

SAM: What?

(KATIE kisses him. He is unresponsive. She takes the bowl, exits into kitchen. She comes back a moment later.)

SAM: Is the doctor at nine or nine-thirty tomorrow?

KATIE: Nine-thirty.

SAM: O K. I'll call Kyle.

KATIE: You've missed two days already. Don't.

(SAM *just stares at her.*)

SAM: How are your ribs? *(Pause)* I can get the pills. You want—

KATIE: I'm fine.

SAM: Are you sure?

(KATIE *nods.*)

SAM: You're sure?

(Pause)

KATIE: I gotta go over to Joymore.

SAM: You're developing tonight?

KATIE: Yeah, plus, I got a lot of framing.

SAM: Sure you're O K with that?

KATIE: Well, I do have to make money and I can't—

SAM: *(Over her)* Don't do the money thing. It's—

KATIE: You know the drill. I develop and frame at night. That's just what happens.

SAM: Not tonight. O K.

(She kisses him.)

KATIE: I love you.

SAM: I know. I know that but—

KATIE: I do, O K. Like really.

SAM: I know.

KATIE: But...?

SAM: But—I don't know—my head is like...

KATIE: You want some Tylenol 3?

SAM: No—it's just...

(KATIE *blasts the C D player. My Bloody Valentine's*
To Here Knows When *plays.* KATIE *dances. It's amazingly
seductive. Tries to touch* SAM. *He's having none of it and
eventually turns off the music.*)

SAM: Well, that helped my headache.

(KATIE *lays down. Long pause*)

KATIE: Lay down, man.

(SAM *lays down. She tries ineffectually to put his arm
around her.*)

KATIE: Let's cuddle.

SAM: You don't cuddle.

(KATIE *throws her other arm around* SAM.)

KATIE: Cuddle Fest! Cuddle-cuddle-cuddle!

(SAM *breaks out of the so-called "cuddle fest".*)

SAM: Get me the Pedialyte.

(KATIE *goes into the bag and gets a thing of Pedialyte.*
SAM *drinks it.*)

SAM: The girl at the counter said it was good because
when you throw up you lose electrolytes.

KATIE: Baby Pedialyte— Good.(*She takes the Pedialyte,
gulps it.*)Boo-ya-ca-cha.

SAM: Nice.

KATIE: Tell me a joke.

SAM: What joke?

KATIE: I don't know. You're The Joke Man.

SAM: You want a joke? O K, so there's this guy.
And this girl. And the girl...gets hurt and the guy's
way of helping her is to throw up all the time.

KATIE: You help me.

SAM: I do?

KATIE: More than anybody ever.

(She kisses him.)

SAM: Don't go out tonight.

KATIE: I like your face when you get serious,
Mister Serious Face.

SAM: Don't.

KATIE: I like your face, motherfucker.

(SAM gets off the bed. Takes out his cellphone)

SAM: I'll call Kyle.

KATIE: Sam, honestly.

SAM: The clinic's in like the worst imaginable part of
town. The doctor's even in a gang, I think. *(Beat)* Plus,
my mom called this morning. They want to come down.

KATIE: NO!!

SAM: They want to help with the wedding.

KATIE: Did you tell them?

(Pause)

SAM: No.

KATIE: Sam—

SAM: I didn't.

KATIE: How soon might they be coming?

SAM: Two weeks.

KATIE: The wedding's not for a month.

SAM: Yeah, she says they want to.

KATIE: It's just—it's gonna be too much, man.
This month is not gonna be—I mean—I don't need
them here like taking me to Ikea or asking me to get
my tattoo's lazerly removed or will I be taking out
the nipple rings and will it effect breast feeding?

SAM: They just want to help.

KATIE: What am I, like an invalid or something?

SAM: I'm just saying.

KATIE: What are you saying?

(Pause. KATIE *grabs her purse.)*

SAM: Where are you going?

KATIE: A week from tomorrow, Sam, I have to load-in
the DeWitt show and I only have like half my stuff.

SAM: So you really need to do photography?

KATIE: Yes.

SAM: Tonight?

KATIE: You're not— The DeWitt is a big show—
like really big—and, as of right now, I have no pictures
to hang.

SAM: What are you talking about? I've seen those
pictures. They're great.

KATIE: They suck. All my new stuff sucks.

SAM: I guess I just—I don't see what the rush is.

KATIE: It's not a rush. It's a routine. I gotta get back to
my—

SAM: Right, but look what happened. Maybe that
routine wasn't—

KATIE: *(Over him)* Look what happened? You're telling
me to look what happened?

SAM: You were in the hospital.

KATIE: *(Pause)* I think I just farted.

(KATIE makes a fart noise. SAM stares.)

KATIE: Would you stop making this tense?

SAM: I'm not making this tense. I'm just—

KATIE: You are, though.

SAM: I'm not. I'm just—I'm saying maybe it's not easy for me like it's easy for you.

KATIE: Just cause I'm trying to make it easy for me doesn't actually make it easy for me!!!!

SAM: I know, I'm sorry, but—

KATIE: Tense!!

SAM: Every time I look at you I see him doing it.

(Immediately, KATIE turns on the music.)

(After repeated unsuccessful attempts to get SAM to dance with her, SAM turns off the music.)

SAM: What if he makes bail?

(KATIE leaves the apartment.)

(SAM gets his coat. Is about to leave when:)

(The phone rings. For a long time.)

(The answering machine picks up. Breathing is heard. Slow and soft and muffled.)

(SAM does not move.)

(Blackout)

Scene Two

(Six A M the next morning, Thursday. SAM *is on the phone.)*

SAM: Danny. Hey, man. It's Sam. Sorry it's so early. Um. Got your message. Um yeah let's definitely meet this morning. Eight A M. Palmer House. I will be there. Um. All right, Danny, talk to you later. *(Calls someone else)* Ellen, hi this is Sam again. Just wondering if Katie's maybe over at your place. She didn't come home last night. Um—just call me and let me know. Bye. 773-385-2929. Bye.

*(*KATIE *comes in.)*

KATIE: You will not believe what happened.

SAM: Probably not.

KATIE: I totally worked until like four in the morning and then I was waiting for the prints to wash and I was waiting and waiting and I like totally fell asleep. In the darkroom. How much does that suck? *(She puts her stuff down. Messes up* SAM*'s hair.)*You were in my dream, though, stud muffin. So that was pretty cool. You were like you still or whatever but you were dressing like one of my friends.

SAM: Which one?

KATIE: Claude.

SAM: Which one's Claude?

KATIE: The one without eyebrows.

SAM: Oh right. Claude.

KATIE: The one with the mohawk.

SAM: Oh, I know Claude.

KATIE: You were dressing like him.

SAM: Like how?

KATIE: Gas attendant shirt, carrying a skateboard.

SAM: Radical.

KATIE: Shut up. Skateboards are cool.

SAM: You talk like your eighteen.

KATIE: I thought you liked that.

SAM: What?

KATIE: Eighteen year olds. Like those interns you always talk about.

SAM: Sooo? I like the high school thing. Taking em back to the copy room. Giving em paper cuts on their naked little rumpies. *(Pause)* Yeah. Rumpies, Katie. That's... the word I used in that last sentence.

(KATIE laughs and pulls SAM down to the bed, where she shoulder-hits him and he winces.)

KATIE: Pussy. *(Pause)* What's a matter?

SAM: Nothing.

KATIE: What's a matter?

SAM: You could have like called.

KATIE: Affirmative.

SAM: I was worried.

KATIE: I was fine.

SAM: I know. I was just—

KATIE: So I'll bring you with next time. It's actually sort of fun sleeping in a darkroom.

SAM: What darkroom did you use?

KATIE: Joymore. Why do you ask?

SAM: I called Joymore. No one picked up.

KATIE: The phone's...not in the darkroom.

SAM: I got an appointment with Sara over at Hunsinger. She said we could see the Orland Park house at one, and then go right over to the Wrigleyville condo at one-forty—if you want.

KATIE: Good transition.

SAM: You still wanna look at the Wrigleyville condo?

KATIE: Yeah, it's cool. It's right near the el and the Beacon Street studio and the Ehlers gallery. It's perfect.

SAM: Yeah, but it's five minutes from here. I mean, if we're gonna move, I want to move away. I don't want to move over.

KATIE: You have this thing for the suburbs, don't you?

SAM: Of course I have a thing for the suburbs. That is where you go to like raise a family.

KATIE: Right, cause there are no families in the city. Burn! Can you call the clinic and tell them I'm not coming in?

SAM: What?

KATIE: Call and cancel. I've got too much work.

SAM: You gotta go. You're not gonna get better.

KATIE: Sam, it's not your vagina.

(SAM *crosses to phone and then stops abruptly.*)

SAM: I called in to work, though. I was gonna take you.

KATIE: Not my fault. I told you not to.

SAM: Yeah, because you never planned on going to the clinic in the first place.

KATIE: *(Over him)* What?

SAM: Which is why you wanted me to go to work— which is why this pisses you off—

KATIE: *(Over him)* What are you mumbling?

SAM: I followed you last night. *(Pause)* Saw you get on the train so I got on train. You got off at Damon, so I got off at Damon but you walked faster than me and why were you walking so fast?

KATIE: Why did you follow me?

SAM: Why did you lie to me? I guess I just don't get the point about lying about this dark room stuff. It's not like I care.

KATIE: You do care, though.

SAM: If I'm getting lied to?

(KATIE kisses him for a long time.)

KATIE: Wanna go to the Cubs game? *(Pause)* Don't fuck around, you know you like baseball.

SAM: Course I like baseball. That's not the—

KATIE: You like Superman still, too, right, or are all your hobbies different all a sudden?

SAM: *(Over "all a sudden")* Superman is not a hobby. Superman is a hero.

KATIE: HA!

SAM: Shut up.

KATIE: No, it's cute. I smiled so much at you the first time you talked about Superman. You were telling me about your theory that Superman's costume was—

SAM: Uniform—

KATIE: Right, his uniform was supposed to be peach, but that F D R made him red, white and blue so he could promote patriotism or something and that's why the villains were always foreigners. Or bald.

SAM: Where did you go last night?

(Pause)

SAM: I mean, Joymore's off the blue line, not the brown line.

KATIE: I went to see Ellen first, O K, before I went the darkroom.

SAM: Ellen? Oh!

KATIE: You don't have to worry. I mean—I don't even—it's not like I feel bad anymore.

SAM: You don't feel bad at all.

(KATIE lifts up her shirt a little bit. SAM starts to kiss her stomach. Stops when he sees teeth marks. And bruises.)

(When SAM touches the teeth marks, KATIE pulls down her shirt. SAM grabs her around the chest; an embrace more than a restraint. He kisses her cheek, releases her.)

SAM: I should go.

KATIE: Thought you called in.

SAM: Yeah, but I still have some...stuff I need to take care of.

KATIE: Are you like in the mafia now?

SAM: My friend Danny, you know? He um—I want him to represent you. He said he's cool with it. Which is great because—um—he's great. Just, you know, a great lawyer. Or whatever.

KATIE: Huh-huh.

SAM: So it's good, right. You're cool with it?

KATIE: With Danny? I mean, isn't it weird or something having our friends involved?

SAM: I already told him yes.

KATIE: *(Pause)* You did.

SAM: Yes. I'm sorry, I want the best.

KATIE: Am I supposed to say thank you?

SAM: No, just—you'll have to say exactly how everything happened. We're gonna need to know it all.

KATIE: We? Are you my lawyer now too?

(SAM *kisses her.*)

SAM: Bye.

KATIE: I'll be here.

SAM: Promise?

KATIE: *(Beat)* You know, I'll even be wifey-wifey and make some Rice-A-Roni. How's that sound?

SAM: Hmmm.

KATIE: And then I'll spill it all over my chest and my legs and you'll have to lick it off— *(Fake moaning)* Oh, Rice-A-Roni-Oh my God, Rice a Roni, The San Francisco treat!

(KATIE *fake writhes on* SAM's *lap. He eventually gets up to go.*)

KATIE: I shouldn't follow you, should I?

(SAM *shakes his head. Leaves*)

Scene Three

(Early Thursday evening. ELLEN *is there with* KATIE.*)*

ELLEN: How do you feel?

(KATIE *gives her a big thumbs-up.*)

ELLEN: You need anything? Tylenol? *(Pause)* Vitamins?

KATIE: Oh my God, stop.

ELLEN: Why can't I help you?

KATIE: Why can't you help me? Are you actually asking me that?

ELLEN: Of course I'm actually—

KATIE: *(Over her)* You come in here, wearing that outfit, like you're actually supposed to fool someone or—

ELLEN: What's wrong with my—

KATIE: *(Over her)* That's a pantsuit! You're wearing a pantsuit!

ELLEN: I know a good psychologist

(KATIE grunts)

ELLEN: No, he's good. I'm not telling you this because I'm worried. I'm telling you this because he's good. He works with artists, a lot, too.

KATIE: Because we're tormented? Because we can't get jobs?

ELLEN: Because you've been raped.

(KATIE stands.)

ELLEN: Please can you just—can you hear me for a second?

ELLEN: Did um—can I ask how it happened?

KATIE: No.

ELLEN: I mean, not like details but just—

KATIE: No. I'll walk you out.

ELLEN: I mean, I know him, you know? He—

KATIE: You don't know him.

ELLEN: I don't know him? That's right, it wasn't me who bailed him out when he stole those acrylics from Ace Hardware for that like ten foot painting of your face. That—

KATIE: And what did he say? Did he ever tell you thanks? He said-

ELLEN: I know what he—

KATIE: *(Over her)* He said to stay out of his life cause you quote "weren't made of anything real!"

ELLEN: How's the wedding stuff?

KATIE: We're good. *(Pause)* Except for uh the caterers who—my friends are all vegan so the cake is gonna taste like goat shit and the tailors who—I went in the other day and found out you and all the bridesmaids' little outfits are all like Cindy Lauper rejects. And the jazz band that cancelled and now we have to hire a D J who'll play M C Hammer all night!

ELLEN: I can go talk to the tailors if you want. There's a way to talk to these people.

KATIE: Nah.

ELLEN: Honey, look, I can do it! You want it a certain way, that's how you get it! It's just being firm with them.

KATIE: No, it just sucks. Mom should be here doing that. She calls me at the hospital saying she "hopes everything's all right". Not "can I come there and help" but—I mean—how can she not come?

ELLEN: I know.
Do you wanna sit?

KATIE: No.

ELLEN: Yes, you do.

(ELLEN leads KATIE to the bed.)

KATIE: You know—something happens to your kid—you go see your kid.

ELLEN: I'll call her.

KATIE: I don't want her here. She'd just be dour and use her unnecessary British accent. *(Pause)* You know, when this whole thing goes through and me and Sam are— you know—it'll be sooo good to say I'm nothing like Mom. Bouncing around to whatever euro-trash passes as companionship in her circle. I swear, I'm not gonna be fifty years old, living in hotels, boasting to my Botox friends about whatever upper crust man I'm trying to, you know, take a bite out of. That W T O thing in London, Mom, not knowing who he was, actually tried to pick up Noam Chomsky. What the fuck is that? I am not going to be that lady!

ELLEN: Me neither.

KATIE: You won't be, I'm sure.

ELLEN: No, I will not.

KATIE: Don't get defensive.

ELLEN: I'm not.

KATIE: *(Pause)* You're like pissed. Your face is all pissed.

ELLEN: Not really.

KATIE: Oh, I get it. Marriage stuff. That's what this is.

ELLEN: Marriage is great. Mars Jupiter compromising. Great.

KATIE: It's O K to be jealous.

ELLEN: What makes you think I'm jealous?

KATIE: 1986. Kenny Ames. The boy next door. You. Him. The tent made out of Care Bears. I mean, not like the hide of Care Bears... And you and Kenny were husband and wife. Ten years old. Playing house. But you took it so seriously, like how you were gonna afford that month's power bill and shit.

ELLEN: So?

KATIE: You were ten years old! That is so fucked up.

ELLEN: You liked him, too. *(Over her)* Oh, yes you did. And he would always avoid you cause you were so young and you always wanted to like wrestle.

KATIE: He did not avoid me.

ELLEN: *(Over her)* Yes, yes he did cause you always wanted to wrestle.

KATIE: Yeah, I was into wrestling back then.

ELLEN: Kenny Ames, my ten year old husband, avoided you, Kate. And you are still bitter.

KATIE: Kenny Ames, I'll say it again, did not avoid me. *(Pause)* In fact, it was quite the opposite summer before high school when he popped me one underneath the deck.

ELLEN: Popped you one? Oh, that's classy.

KATIE: I'm just saying he didn't avoid me.

ELLEN: And I'm saying classy. *(Pause)* Did you really have sex with him?

KATIE: Blame Kenny, man. All I did was lay there.

(ELLEN stands, goes to her purse.)

ELLEN: I have Sam's cellphone number. Just tell him I'll call him later?

KATIE: What did you just say?

ELLEN: I said be nicer to me.

KATIE: How did you get his number?

ELLEN: He called me before. I just have to call him back. *(She starts to leave.)*

KATIE: Wait. I'm sorry.

(KATIE cuts off ELLEN at the door.)

KATIE: I'm like kicking you out. We didn't even talk. I mean, not really. Not about...how school is. How's school?

ELLEN: Are you being nice?

(KATIE sits ELLEN down at the table.)

ELLEN: School is good. I mean, if you like ten hours of lab work where all you do is listen to children repeat nonsense syllables just so my professor really knows I really understand the "experimental" psychology of Hermann Ebbinghaus. I don't wanna bore you.

KATIE: You're not.

ELLEN: It's just science stuff.

KATIE: I know.

ELLEN: It's like complicated.

KATIE: Well, contrary to public belief, I am not a monkey.

ELLEN: How are your pictures coming?

(Pause)

ELLEN: I guess I'll go then. Paperwork awaits. Thanks for being nice to me.

KATIE: I need a favor.

ELLEN: *(Pause)* ...O K.

KATIE: I told Sam I went to see you last night.

ELLEN: But you didn't.

KATIE: Exactly.

ELLEN: O K. Well, where did you go? *(Pause)* O K.

KATIE: You're not gonna um—you know—

ELLEN: Call Sam? Don't worry, I know I'm on Sam probation. (*She comes close to* KATIE.) I'm just trying to help you, you know.

KATIE: O K.

ELLEN: You know you need it.

KATIE: O K.

(ELLEN *hugs* KATIE.)

KATIE: Please stay away.

(*Blackout*)

Scene Four

(*Friday, 5:30 P M.* KATIE's *lights are set-up for a photo session. There is wine all around.*)

(SAM *comes in, wearing a tie and carrying a briefcase and a Wal-Mart bag.*)

KATIE: Hello, honey.

SAM: What is this?

KATIE: Stuff. Lights. Camera. Action. You know.

SAM: Kinda bright, wouldn't you say?

KATIE: I would say that, yeah. Kinda bright. Can I kiss you?

(KATIE *kisses* SAM.)

SAM: Does this mean that a model's coming over and that I gotta leave?

KATIE: No, it's you.

SAM: What?

KATIE: It's you. I'm taking pictures of you.

SAM: Why?

(KATIE sets down SAM's Wal-Mart bag.)

KATIE: Because we're getting married, Mister Wal-Mart.

SAM: Oh and this is part of the deal, huh? I have to become a, a stud model person or something?

KATIE: Models aren't studs. Models are people you take pictures of.

SAM: Know something, now that I think about it, people have always taken pictures of me.

SAM: Yeah, most people I know have a picture of me on their fridge. Not because they like me. But because they don't want to forget me. And they would, without the picture.

KATIE: I don't forget you. Ever.

SAM: Yeah, but it's different. I pay you.

KATIE: Shut up. Sit down and be a stud model person.

(SAM sits down and does a few poses as KATIE starts taking pictures of him. After a few shots, she speaks:)

KATIE: You called Ellen. When I was in the hospital. Which is weird—

SAM: Sisters come to this type of thing. They—

KATIE: Not if you don't call them they don't.

SAM: How could I not call her? Come on.

KATIE: You come on first and tell me how you got her number. *(Pause)* Tell me.

SAM: *(Speaks over "Tell me")* Your cellphone.

KATIE: Oh, my cellphone? How vewy intewesting.

SAM: I had to, O K, it was—

KATIE: No, what you had to do was mind your own business.

SAM: Sorry.

KATIE: Don't do it again.

SAM: *(Pause)* Though I don't get why there's this restraining order on your sister—

KATIE: We're not talking about this—

SAM: It was a Christmas party! You were drunk, too, O K—

KATIE: *(Under him)* Oh my God.

SAM: And, oh my God, Ellen ran her mouth off and so what? She ran her mouth off. That's what you do at Christmas parties.

KATIE: No, you run your mouth off—fine—do it about yourself! Not about other people cause other people don't liked to be talked about all the time.

SAM: You don't?

(KATIE runs her hands through SAM's hair.)

KATIE: Sam-Sam-Sammy pie. *(Pause)* What did you wanna do today? Did you wanna leave, stay, keep working, what?

SAM: Actually, yeah, I was making some strides, teaching a couple interns this C plus plus program.

KATIE: Oh, you and your interns. Did you wanna stick your hand inside? Inside their, you know, hard drive?

SAM: Um—

KATIE: Do you touch the right button most of the time or is it like you have to finger around for a while, you know, get the groove?

SAM: You're drunk.

KATIE: Nope. Just funny.

SAM: God. It's five-thirty, Katie.

KATIE: When you're at work, do you get like—do you ever sit at your desk and look at your picture of me and wanna just get up and leave and come be with me and run through the wheatgrass with me?

SAM: Yep. Exactly.

(KATIE hits him in the chest.)

KATIE: Don't placate me! This is real what I'm talking about! This is what makes me like itch myself at eight o'clock in the morning. When you wake up for work and think I'm still sleeping- Yeah, I just get this itching thing going on and I scratch up my skin and I try to bleed enough so that the blood pool in the bed will get as big as you.

SAM: You are so drunk, oh my God!

KATIE: No, man, I'm being dramatic! And then you know what I think? And it's more like a fart kind of, then a thought, But you know what I think?
I think about you doing things at work that you never do.

SAM: Like what?

KATIE: Like me.

SAM: I never do you at work?

KATIE: No, not even in your head. Since you're so good at your work and you get promotions more than I get mail, I know that you don't do me at work. I know that you work at work.

SAM: I'm sorry.

(KATIE straddles SAM.)

KATIE: Don't be sorry! Be creative. Make something up, man. Tell me some bullshit stories about how hard it is to finger those computers cause you miss me so bad.

SAM: What are these pictures for?

KATIE: Church lobby.

SAM: I don't want weird pictures at my wedding. Sorry.

KATIE: *(Hitting him)* You are such a Nazi communist father person sometimes, Sam, I swear to God.

SAM: Yeah, and who knows more about Ansel Adams than you ever will?

KATIE: Because you took a class?

SAM: I'm not doing this.

KATIE: Doing what? Fighting. Marrying me in a month? What, Sam?

SAM: I'm not being the person you yell at.

KATIE: Be the person I want then.

SAM: How?

KATIE: Show me you want me.

SAM: I want you.

KATIE: Then fuck me.

(SAM crosses to her, stops, then crosses to door.)

KATIE: Fuck you. What's hard about this for you? You're not gonna go through this making me look like the asshole. Like I need you here to comfort me— cause what I need—Sam—LOOK AT ME—

(SAM turns around.)

KATIE: Tell me why you're the guy. Why I should stop things—put a pause on what I'm doing and marry you and get kids and have you when I—

SAM: No. I'm outta this. I'm not here to pitch myself to you. Cause you knew— Cause you knew—when I was there—that first night with you—that was it— that was me. And cause I'm the only one around here who doesn't fuck around with himself and make himself this big deal for everybody to see how I can just, you know, flaunt it and say you don't know the first thing about me. Well, I tell you something, you do. You know the first thing. Cause I give it to you cause that's just me. I meet somebody and, hey, I want em to know me. Am I so off the fucking mark? I almost got fired today. I was checking my Hotmail and this is all gonna sound made-up but there was a junk mail message to me and the subject line was, "Do you like it rough?" So, I'm figuring, sure, I have about an hour before I have to work, I'll look at some porn. It's—the first video—it's this girl tied down to a chain-link fence and a guy in a Ken mask like a mask based on Ken and Barbie—and he's just...having his way with this girl. But that's not the disturbing thing. The disturbing thing is—the girl's like enjoying it. She—so I like kick my computer—I kick it—and it must have been the angle or something—but I like really fucked up my toe. And so I make this noise—like a pain noise—and by this point people are filing into their cubicles and they all look into my cubicle and they see this vicious porn and they see me hunched over and moaning. Needless, to say, Leonard told me to go home for the day, after explaining in detail the company's policy about masturbation in the work place. So I leave and I have this whole day to fill. And I find myself at a pay phone, looking through the phone book and for some reason, I stop when I come to "Private Detectives."

(Long pause.)

SAM: I spent a lot of money today. By a lot I mean in the thousands. I met with this guy: Michael T Radivick, told him this was work I wanted done pronto and, Jesus, it didn't take him ten minutes to get the address. And two minutes to jimmy the door.

(SAM takes a small portrait from his briefcase. It's of KATIE. Her arms across a bare chest. It's stunning.)

SAM: When did he paint this? *(Pause)* When?! *(Pause)*
You know what the last thing I did today was?
I wanted it to be so much more dramatic. Like me
going over there and causing this big scene and
gutting this apartment and just—you know—*blitzkrieg.*
But what did I do? I knocked a towel off his towel rack.
How bout that for revenge?

(KATIE starts to speak.)

SAM: Why were you there? *(He takes out his cellphone.)*

SAM: Danny needs to know— He left a message.
Here—listen—

(SAM offers her his cellphone.)

KATIE: What do you want?

SAM: I want you.

KATIE: No you don't.

SAM: That's why I went there!

KATIE: No, why you went there is cause you think
there's some mystery to solve and now you're like this
private detective—

SAM: It is a mystery to me! Not why I was there
but why you were there. *(He gives her the painting.)*
Bring it back. If you want. Apartment's gonna be
confiscated, might as well use it while you can.
Since you have a spare key, I take it. Oh and nice
dark room he's got there, huh? He build that for you?

(Long pause)

KATIE: I was raped.

(Blackout)

Scene Five

(Saturday. ELLEN *is there with* SAM, *who looks more disheveled.)*

ELLEN: He's a painter.

SAM: I know and—she what—she loved him—what?

ELLEN: One time, He was away at Yale—

SAM: He went to Yale?

ELLEN: Yeah.

SAM: I didn't even get into Yale.

ELLEN: He's bright.

SAM: You think?!!!

ELLEN: Oh, and let's see, he does modeling stuff.

SAM: Like in his underwear stuff?

ELLEN: Yeah, you've seen em. They're on the side of city buses.

SAM: O K stop.

ELLEN: And he proposed to her twice, but she kept saying no.

SAM: Why?

ELLEN: He um...he gets bad sometimes. Like one time Katie went to New York to see this Joyce Tenneson exhibit and he didn't want her to go and so he actually went down there, got into her hotel room, piled all the furniture in front of the door so they couldn't get out and they stayed there. Holed up for five days in which time He got liver poisoning because he drank and wouldn't stop drinking until Katie promised never to leave him again.

*(*SAM *says nothing.)*

ELLEN: It's weird. Cause right when I saw him for the first time and, even in high school, together, the two of them were like—

SAM: Has she been seeing him the whole time she's been with me?

ELLEN: Why do you think Katie wanted an unlisted phone number? Why do you think she was like more than eager to get out of her old place and move in with you?

SAM: Sounds like the witness protection program.

ELLEN: She was trying to cut him off, Sam. And, for a whole year, she did.

ELLEN: Then, somehow he got this number. Somehow he hunted her down. Like he always said he would.

(Noise in the hallway. SAM *checks the peephole, opens the door and checks down the hall.)*

ELLEN: Is it her?

SAM: No, there's no one. *(He closes door.)* Five years. At the Christmas party you said they were together for five years.

ELLEN: *(Pause)* Ah, that fated Christmas party. That is what I said, yes. Five years. Which is why I shouldn't be doing this.

SAM: You have to do this. I cannot. These questions— what am I supposed to do—I can't ask Katie these questions.

ELLEN: Maybe you should.

SAM: *(Over her)* This won't be an open and shut case! Don't you get that? It's gonna be bad, O K, because I need—my lawyer needs—like testimony from you, from somebody about who these two people are. They found a camera. They said they think he...took pictures of her while he was... doing it. But he must have destroyed the film. They can't find the film. There's no evidence. Of anything. Other than sex.

ELLEN: Evidence? She was in the hospital. She has like bruised ribs.

(Pause. SAM *is momentarily caught in his lie.)*

SAM: Wednesday night. Did Katie go to your place on Wednesday night?

*(*ELLEN *doesn't answer.)*

SAM: I knew it. Why the hell would she go back there?

ELLEN: She's just going through withdrawal.

SAM: Going through withdrawal? She's going back to the scene of the crime is what she's doing. Couldn't she like tamper with shit? I mean, what the fuck is that?

*(*ELLEN *stands.)*

ELLEN: I should probably go. There's just all this crap schoolwork I have to do, that I have been doing since like six this morning. Re-reading Sigmund again: The Psychopathology of Everyday Life. It's great the first ten times but—

SAM: I like in the end where he talks about man being jealous of the actions he never takes. *(Pause)* It's good you took action. I need to like um... *(Pause)* I mean about you going to grad school and—

ELLEN: I've got a secret. Cause I met you like right before I applied—but I never told you that you were like—don't laugh at me—but you were one of the reasons I applied. Cause—yeah, cause I saw you— I mean—you had your masters at twenty-six and there I was at twenty-nine and what I'm saying is—I don't know what I'm saying.

SAM: I'll take it as a compliment.

ELLEN: Cool.

(Pause)

SAM: Cause I need a compliment.

ELLEN: Here's another one then. While I'm—whatever—feeling magnanimous. I think you'll be a great husband. No, really. I um—it's so impressive I think what you've done at this age. Like how long did it take you to get V P of E Commerce? A year?

SAM: Nine months. A company car, too, but who's counting?

(They laugh.)

ELLEN: It's nice when you smile.

SAM: *(Pause)* O K so by your estimation, if I became C E O and Chairman of the board by—let's say—the time I'm forty, does that catapult me to—

ELLEN: Perfect husband, you got it!

SAM: Awesome.

ELLEN: Awesome. Not that your wife will care.

SAM: Well, that's good.

ELLEN: I mean Katie cares, but only as much as like... a heroin addict cares for methadone.

SAM: You don't like her much. Do you? Like at all?

ELLEN: No. I love her—

SAM: Mmm-huh.

ELLEN: I just think—perhaps she's not cut out for this. You. This. Marriage.

SAM: You just said I'd be a great husband. Are you saying—what are you saying?

(ELLEN crosses and sits next to SAM. Long pause)

SAM: Am I good, Ellen?

ELLEN: Yes.

(SAM *removes contents of Wal-Mart bag: mace,
A D T Home Security Unit, nunchucks and a taser gun.*)

SAM: *(Under his breath, as he takes out the items)* Mace.
A D T Home Security Unit. Nunchucks. Taser.

(SAM *and* ELLEN *stare at the Wal-Mart arsenal.*)

SAM: I feel bad.

(Blackout)

Scene Six

(8:30 P M, that night. SAM *is drunk, he is sitting in the dark
with a bottle of whiskey and an empty can of Spagettii-O's.*)

(KATIE *enters.* SAM *clicks on lamp.*)

SAM: Lights. Camera. Action. Look what I got.

(SAM *shows* KATIE *his new, disposable camera, pretending to
do a photo session.*)

KATIE: Cute.

SAM: Hmm-hmm. And disposable. I must say I could
really get used to this whole artist thing. Today was
awesome! Laying round the house, drinking, just
looking at things. Much better for me, I think.
Computers, computers—blah—who wants that?

KATIE: What are you talking about?

SAM: *(Pedantic)* My art, honey. I'm talking about my art.
But I knew you wouldn't care. No one does. I've got
pain, o.k, pain. I need to create. Not at eight in the
morning, of course, but I do need to! But definitely
no nine-to-five stop and start. My art comes when it

comes. And, if it doesn't, fuck it. I'll just... Uh-oh
spaghetti-O's

KATIE: Good impression. Don't think you made me
lazy enough, but we can work on that.

(SAM *gives her a thumbs-up.*)

KATIE: Plus you made the camera thing too hard.
All you gotta do is put in the film, point, shoot and
there you have it! And when you want to develop,
all you gotta do is booze it on up. Press this here
button near your back side, and then, presto! Photos
come out your asshole! Oh and backlight doesn't
matter. Overexposure. Shutter speed. All art is good art.
Fuck, I mean Weston shot "The Last Years in Carmel"
just by drinking moonshine!

SAM: I think you have potential.

KATIE: Are you fucking kidding me?

SAM: Yes.

KATIE: You think it's that easy?

SAM: No.

KATIE: Photography.

SAM: I don't know.

KATIE: You do.

SAM: I don't.

KATIE: You do.

SAM: I don't! I do not know! You never give me a
chance to see.

KATIE: It's my life, Sam, you don't need a chance to see
it.

(SAM *does a nunchuck demonstration. As hard as he tries,
he's too drunk to be good.*)

SAM: Ellen says hi.
I followed you this morning Of course. Walking fast.
Again. I wanted to be you, again. Thinking if I could
just have whatever balls you have—then I could do
something I want to do for once instead of— But I tried
and tried and I went to Wal-Mart yesterday. So all day
I've been trying to install the A D T home security unit,
but it went off and wouldn't stop going off, so I
basically went deaf and had to rip it off the wall.
I bought this mace and this tazer gun, and so I tazered
the bed, but it goy caught on the sheets, and I like
totally ruined the comforter. Yippee for Sam! Here!
I bought you a safety whistle.

(SAM *puts the safety whistle on* KATIE.)

KATIE: You shouldn't have talked to Ellen.

SAM: You shouldn't have made me. What, like I wanted
to know about him going to Yale or like locking you up
in some Holiday Inn!

KATIE: *(Underneath "proposing")* Sam—

SAM: You go to his apartment!!

KATIE: So do you.

SAM: You go more than me.

(SAM *and* KATIE *struggle. End in rough embrace on ground)*

SAM: Don't go to his place anymore.

KATIE: I'll stop if you stop.

SAM: I am trying to stop. We convict him, it stops.
We need more. One more nail. In the coffin. This guy
is dead. We'll move where ever you want to move.
Apartment, house, I don't care. I just want to live in the
same place you live.

KATIE: *(Pause)* How bout a picket fence?

SAM: I'll paint it myself.

KATIE: Like that retarded kid from that book?

SAM: *(Pause)* Tom Sawyer?

KATIE: Yeah.

SAM: I don't think Tom Sawyer was retarded.

KATIE: Oh.

SAM: But, yes. Exactly. I'll be like him.

KATIE: And then...

SAM: I'll do something my mom told me about which is this: I asked her when I was a kid how kids were like made. And she said that the daddy and the mommy kiss so much that their lips fall off and combine together to make the shape of a baby.

KATIE: That's really fucked up.

SAM: I love you. But I need to know more.

KATIE: No, Sam, you don't.

(The phone rings two times. The answering machine picks up—there is a piercing dial tone.)

(SAM looks at KATIE.)

(Blackout)

Scene Seven

(Sunday, 4:30 P M)

(KATIE enters with a black portfolio.)

KATIE: Sam?*(She pokes her head into the hallway.)*Sam. *(She climbs a chair and hides the portfolio in the overhead soffit.)*

(Someone rings the buzzer.)

KATIE: Hello?

(KATIE *presses the intercom. We hear the outside world.*
KATIE *walks away.*)

(*The buzzer rings again.*)

KATIE: Hello?

(*We again hear the outside world.* KATIE *walks away.*)

(*For a third time, The buzzer rings. Louder and longer than before.*)

KATIE: Hello?!!

(*This time, we hear My Bloody Valentine's* To Here Knows When *playing in the distant soundscape.*)

(KATIE, *freaked out, goes and grabs the baseball bat.*)

(*The second she turns around,* ELLEN *opens the front door. They both scream.* ELLEN *is holding a box of Franzia.*)

ELLEN: I have a box of Franzia.

KATIE: O K.

ELLEN: We can drink it. Sam invited me over for dinner.

KATIE: He did?

ELLEN: Yes. How about you put the bat down?
So, aren't you going to invite me in?

(KATIE *puts down bat.* ELLEN *goes to kitchen and gets wine glasses. While* ELLEN's *in the kitchen,* KATIE *looks at the over-head soffet to make sure the portfolio is safely hidden.*)

KATIE: Did you actually buy wine that comes in a box?

ELLEN: Believe or not, the University of Chicago likes it when you repay your student loans. So, yes, my budget includes boxed wine.(*She comes back from the kitchen.*)Where's Sam?

(KATIE *doesn't answer.*)

ELLEN: (*Pause*) Mom called this morning. And, she was being so stupid, I swear. She said, "Tell Katie she has no

business getting married." And I was like "Mom, first
of all, why do you have an accent? And, second of all,
Katie's business is Katie's business and she doesn't like
it when—

KATIE: You're right. I don't.

ELLEN: But what I'm thinking is Mom has a point.
I mean just about maybe postponing the wedding.
You know, for right now. Toast.

KATIE: When's the last time you went on a date?

ELLEN: E-Harmony dot com. I go on dates all the time.

KATIE: Your personal profile says and I quote "Looking
for a man who is not afraid of marriage, children or the
novels of Nicholas Sparks". You do not go on dates.

ELLEN: Men are scared of commitment.

KATIE: Men are scared of you.

ELLEN: I think you're taking it out on me. Your anger.

KATIE: What anger?

ELLEN: You used to always talk about your pictures,
like all day every day. It was everything to you.
But now it's like nothing. And I think you're angry.

(Pause. ELLEN *takes off her coat.)*

ELLEN: Of course you're angry. Every single picture
you've produced this year is a piece of flailing shit.

KATIE: Wow.

ELLEN: There's nothing real in it. In any of it. They're
just these like Norman Rockwell safe-zones and
everything's tidy and everything makes sense and
there is no feeling of—aahh—you might as well be
taking high school portraits. But that's not why you're
angry. You're angry because every single picture
you've produced this year has sold. Every single gallery

that rejected your old stuff for being quote "Too wild to look at" —they're all begging you for more. They just love how you've toned it down and made yourself commercial. But you haven't made yourself anything. You just can't do what you used to do and what you do now you hate. Perhaps Sam just isn't the muse that James was.

KATIE: Thank you, Doctor Phil.

ELLEN: That's not funny. That's a good show. He's a good man.

KATIE: Did you give James this number?

(SAM *enters, hiding a Toys-R-Us bag.*)

ELLEN: The Rose excavation in England. These archeologists found these little ancient cue cards that all had the same weird crease down the middle. Sam, how are you? Turns out Shakespeare's actors would hold the card in between their fingers and that way they knew which speech was coming next.

(Pause)

KATIE: Isn't Ellen so vewy smawt?

ELLEN: *Como estas?*

SAM: Uhm...

KATIE: Shut up, Sam.

ELLEN: Don't tell him to shut up. Jesus.

KATIE: You shut up.

ELLEN: You shut up

KATIE: Shut up.

ELLEN: Shut up!

KATIE: You shut up!

ELLEN: *(Loud) Cayate!*

(SAM *leads* ELLEN *to the table, where the two of them sit down.*)

SAM: Shakespeare!!! Mmm...gotta love Shakespeare. I act out the sonnets from time to time, Ellen. Tights, codpiece, everything. Katie gets kinda sick, so it's more of a "once a year" type a thing.

ELLEN: I'd love to see you as an actor.

SAM: You could have! In college, I had a buddy doing that and he was trying to get me to switch so I signed up for like Acting 101 and—

KATIE: You did not. Could we stop?

SAM: I did but it's not like it lasted cause the first day the teacher told me to feel the energy when I all I wanted to do was like be in a play and not have some major transcendental breakthrough. Um.

KATIE: Tell Ellen what else you did.

(*Pause*)

SAM: No.

KATIE: Come on, Sam.

(SAM *looks at* KATIE.)

KATIE: It's baseball. Sam played baseball.

ELLEN: You did?

KATIE: Yeah, like five years ago. Made varsity as a walk-on.

ELLEN: How come I don't know that?

KATIE: You don't? Weird. You know everything else there is to know about everything ever.

ELLEN: Wow, wow, wow. Katie keeps you hid. Here you are, Mister All-American, and I would have never guessed.

KATIE: Yep, Mister American—playing baseball his whole life 'til he finds out what money is.

SAM: No, I always knew what money was—I just didn't know it could buy so many frigging D V Ds.

(SAM *and* ELLEN *laugh.*)

KATIE: Sam walks on to the varsity baseball team, right—loves it, loves every day of it. Makes all conference 'cause he pitches like three no hitters. But instead of trying for the pros—

SAM: Stop—

KATIE: But instead of trying for the pros, he cashes out and studies computers.

SAM: *(To* ELLEN*)* Minor league players get two hundred a week; it's pretty ridiculous. *(Pause)* But, yes, I always wanted to be an actor, too. Actors are um—they uh...

ELLEN: Didn't James do a play in high school?

(KATIE *starts to leaves the apartment.*)

SAM: Where are you going!

KATIE: *(from the hallway)* No stay with your buddy, Ellen. You can be lil' buddies together. Bye lil' buddies. *(She exits.)*

(SAM *almost follows, hesitates.*)

ELLEN: *(Pause)* I can't believe I said that.

SAM: That was bad.

ELLEN: I'm sorry.

SAM: That was really bad.

ELLEN: God, I think—every time I come here— this happens and I think you guys think I'm this meddling weirdo or something.

SAM: Yeah, um—

ELLEN: *(Over him)* But what's weird is when helping people feels out of place, you know? I mean, am I overstepping my uh, you know, my boundaries here or—

SAM: Maybe but—

ELLEN: Cause my whole thing is I'm really into honesty. And some people *(i.e. her)* really get shocked when I say stuff sometimes.

SAM: It's just your sense of timing is sometimes sort of off.

ELLEN: But at least I'm honest when I say it's too soon for you guys to get married.

(SAM *grabs his coat.*)

ELLEN: Is it getting better? Like have you stopped following her?

SAM: I did something bad this afternoon.

ELLEN: What, Sam?

(SAM *hangs up his coat.*)

SAM: Do you want some more wine?

ELLEN: Sure, I'll have some more wine cause that's exactly what I need right now is more wine.

(SAM *pours her a glass of wine.*)

SAM: Can I tell you something and have you promise not to freak out.

ELLEN: Of course.

SAM: Promise.

ELLEN: I promise, Sam.

SAM: Do you wanna play a game?

(SAM *gets the Toys-R-Us bag. Takes out a plastic Ken mask [based on Ken from Ken and Barbie]. It has a blank smile and painted-on blond hair.)*

SAM: Toys-R-Us. Five ninety-nine. Strange enough, it's kind of actually accurate. His eyes are bluer but.

(SAM *takes out index cards from his pocket, hands them to* ELLEN.)

SAM: I had to write down the questions cause I thought maybe I'd get nervous and I did get nervous so they came in handy. *(Pause)* Just go ahead whenever you're ready.

(SAM *puts on the Ken mask. His whole physicality changes. He becomes stolid and still.)*

ELLEN: Wait, what is going on right now? *(Pause)* Sam?

(SAM *doesn't answer.)*

ELLEN: OK, take that off. This is like creepy.

(SAM *doesn't answer.)*

ELLEN: Take it off, Sam. I'm serious.

(SAM *slowly approaches her, points at the index card.)*

ELLEN: No.

(SAM *puts his masked face near her face. She's scared into compliance. Reads an index card.)*

ELLEN: Um...I know the answer to this already but— O K. *(Reading card)* Is it true you met in high school?

(SAM *nods slightly.)*

ELLEN: *(Reading card)* Is it true you were together for five years?

(SAM *nods slightly.)*

ELLEN: *(Reading card)* Then Katie wanted to end it? But you wouldn't let her? Why wouldn't you let her, James?

(SAM stares.)

ELLEN: *(Reading card)* As someone who went to a state school, I'm curious did you like Yale?

(SAM stares.)

ELLEN: *(Reading card)* I detected a hint of—you spelled Fauvism wrong—I detected a hint of Fauvism in your paintings. How would you classify them, James? Or would you?

(SAM stares.)

ELLEN: *(Reading card)* Are you the one prank calling our apartment? Do the guards let you make phone calls?

(SAM stares.)

ELLEN: *(Putting the cards down)* This is weird, I'm—

(SAM advances.)

ELLEN: It's weird, Sam.

(SAM intimidates her into more.)

ELLEN: *(Picking up the cards)* Did you know Katie and I got engaged?

(SAM nods.)

ELLEN: Did you think she was happy?

(SAM nods.)

ELLEN: Then why did you rape her?

(ELLEN puts down the cards. SAM takes off the mask.)

(Long pause)

SAM: He did that. Today. He stood there—just like that—at prison—behind the glass. His eyes—they were made of nothing. I was made of nothing. No matter what I did. If I yelled at him, punched through the glass and killed him. None of it would have mattered. James...isn't the type of person who dies.

(Pause. KATIE *comes in with a rose. Presents the rose to* SAM. *They do a prom like dance in front of* ELLEN. SAM *pushes away, exits with Ken mask in bag.)*

ELLEN: He's going to leave you.

*(*KATIE *stares at her.)*

KATIE: He said this to you?

ELLEN: Yes.

KATIE: He said it how? How did he say it?

ELLEN: He said, I am going to leave her.

KATIE: Fuck you.

*(*ELLEN *gathers her stuff. Grabs everything but her keys)*

ELLEN: I don't care what has happened between us or what will ever happen between us. You're the only family I have. *(She leaves.)*

*(*KATIE *stands on the chair, removes the black portfolio of pictures. At that instant,* ELLEN *opens the door. At that instant,* KATIE *lets out a surprised shriek.)*

ELLEN: *(Under* KATIE'*s scream)* I forgot my keys. *(She stares at the portfolio.)*

(Blackout)

Scene Eight

(3:00 A M. Monday morning. KATIE *has a bottle of whiskey, a bottle of beer, and a bottle of pills as* SAM *enters from outside with the Ken mask in the bag.)*

KATIE: *(Waking)* Oh, hi.

SAM: Hi.

KATIE: What time is it?

SAM: Three.

KATIE: What happened?

SAM: Come again?

KATIE: What happened?

SAM: I uh—

KATIE: Sam.

SAM: Yeah.

KATIE: What happened?

SAM: Maisie. Maisie happened.

KATIE: Who's Maisie?

SAM: Nobody, don't worry. *(Pause)* A prostitute.

KATIE: Sam—

SAM: Ah, ah, ah! Didn't touch her! Not once!

KATIE: God!

SAM: Her name was Maisie, O K, I had to go with her. Yeah, always been a fan of the southern belle thing, you know? And she just had this drawl in her voice, this lemonade drawl, that made me think of a porch in Georgia. Antebellum kind of stuff. We went back to this joint called The Saint's Place and it was dirty and really bright with yellow, like a Dick Tracy book. Everyone was unshaved. Men, women, the in-betweens. And so many people had lazy eyes, I never knew where to look! But so we go up to her room, Maisie's that is, and she's thinking I'm there to screw her. But right away I tell her "look, Maisie, hands off, I'm getting married. Her name's Katie. Here's her picture." Yeah, the one from my wallet and I stuck it on her wall with some gum! Maisie goes nuts! Looking at the picture, looking at me. Looking at the picture, looking at me. Oh my god. What's he gonna do? And, I don't know. I do not know what I'm going to do. Here, let's have you play Maisie and you're sitting right there on the bed

just—you're staring at me, staring like what's on the
agenda? And hell if I know. So I look at the floor—
and there's a big blue almanac. In this prostitute's
room! And, I'm like "yes, here's something I know!"
I'll just show her I have the capitals memorized!
But she's not paying attention—she's looking at your
picture cause it's so pretty. And so for two hours this
is what I do! I rip off the picture, put it in Maisie's face
and go through the capitals in the almanac. All fifty of
'em. And for each, I say "O K, Boise, Idaho. Give me
a word that starts with B to describe the girl in this
picture." And, of course, that was an easy one and she
goes "beautiful". So, we're off to a good start. But, then
I tell her she can't use the same word twice. Maisie gets
nervous and starts stuttering around, blah-blah, you
know "stop it, I'm scared" all that type of stuff. And,
when we get to Springfield and she's already said
"special" and "sweet", she doesn't know what to say.
So—she rips out some of her pubic hair. That's what
she had to do if she didn't find a word.

KATIE: Why?

SAM: Because I made her!*(He takes the safety whistle from
his pocket.)*Look what I found. You just can't stop going,
there can you?

(KATIE says nothing.)

During the day, you know what I do? You know
Sherlock Holmes? I do the kind of stuff he does.
I'm thinking about even enlisting your sister as Watson.
To investigate me. That's right. Myself! Because I've
been acting—I've gotta admit—a little suspicious and
perhaps even gay. You see, Kate, there's this man that
I...like to think about.

KATIE: Are you leaving me?

SAM: I saw him today. In prison.

KATIE: *(Pause)* You left me tonight. I was here alone.
With Ellen. And I lost it, O K In twenty five years,
I have never cried in front of my sister. You know
what you said about one more nail in the coffin?
That's something I have. *(Pause)* I have the nail, Sam.

(SAM *takes a step toward her.*)

SAM: What is it?

KATIE: Evidence.

SAM: What evidence?

KATIE: Doesn't matter.

SAM: It matters.

KATIE: It's something you don't want to see.

SAM: Of course I wanna see it. If it's evidence, I—

KATIE: You don't want to see it.
Feel me.

SAM: I can't.

KATIE: Why not?

SAM: Cause he felt you, too.

KATIE: He's not here now.

(SAM *looks at the bag that has the Ken mask in it.*)

SAM: Yes he is.

(Blackout)

Scene Nine

(Monday. ELLEN *is there with* SAM.*)*

SAM: I'm gonna leave Katie.

ELLEN: *(Long pause)* Wow.

SAM: Do you think that's O K?

ELLEN: I...don't know what I think.

SAM: I think you're beautiful, Ellen. I think you're smart and I think you're a whole lot more like me than Katie could ever be.

ELLEN: What are you saying?

SAM: I'm saying: me and you.

ELLEN: Are you serious?

SAM: Look at me.

ELLEN: You do look pretty serious.

SAM: I am.

ELLEN: You're like those one of those guards at Buckingham Palace.

SAM: I am like one of those.

ELLEN: And those guys are pretty serious.

(SAM *unzips* ELLEN's *sweater.* SAM *kisses* ELLEN.

(SAM *turns on music. My Bloody Valentine's* To Here Knows When. ELLEN *does a dance like* KATIE. *She looks like* KATIE.)

(SAM *watches for too long, then dances with her. It's slow and sultry and, for once in* SAM's *life, senseless.*)

(ELLEN *goes to her knees, undoes* SAM's *belt.*)

(*Then,* SAM *pulls away. Turns off the music.*)

ELLEN: What?

SAM: What did she show you last night?

(ELLEN *recoils. Knowing she's been used*)

SAM: She said I'm not gonna see whatever this thing is. This evidence. She said I can't see it. Ever. (*He touches* ELLEN's *face.*)What did she show you?

(ELLEN *removes* SAM's *hand from her face, hesitates, then:*)

(ELLEN *gets a chair, stands on it and reaches up to the soffet. It takes a while, but* ELLEN *pulls out the black portfolio.*)

(ELLEN *hands the portfolio to* SAM, *who looks through the pictures, which the audience DOES NOT see.*)

(*As if the wind has been knocked out of him,* SAM *implodes onto the bed.*)

(*After looking at the pictures,* SAM *clutches the portfolio to his chest and starts to hyperventilate.*)

(KATIE *enters.*)

(SAM *bolts up to standing and buckles his belt.*)

(*No one moves.*)

(*Casually,* ELLEN *gathers her things. Leaves*)

(*Long pause*)

KATIE: I was gonna give them to Danny. Tomorrow. By myself.

SAM: Danny didn't need them, Kate. I did. (*Pause*) Why were you there?

KATIE: I did it for you.

SAM: What does that mean?

KATIE: It means he found me. After a year, he finally found our number and it was only a matter of time before he found out where we lived. You have no idea...what he's capable of.

SAM: I get the picture.

KATIE: I had to go to him, Sam. To his apartment. Before he came to ours.

SAM: But you knew. You knew he was gonna...

KATIE: He's gone now, Sam.

SAM: He's not gone. *(He takes out the Ken mask. Does not put it on yet, though)*

KATIE: What are you doing?

SAM: Don't I at least deserve a re-enactment?

KATIE: I don't want to do this.

SAM: You already did this. Without me. I need to go through what you went through...and then we will be through this.

(In the silence, there is a tacit agreement.)

SAM: The lights change and we are in James' apartment. *(He dims the lights. Only moonlight comes in. Barely)* Whenever you're ready.

KATIE: So I walk into his place—

SAM: So do it.

(KATIE leaves the apartment and comes back in.)

KATIE: So I walk into his place—

SAM: Where is he?

KATIE: He has his back to me and he's painting.

(SAM puts on the James mask, turns his back to KATIE and paints the wall.)

KATIE: And without turning, he knows it's me. He says, "Where have you been hiding?"

SAM: Where have you been hiding?

KATIE: And I tell him about you. About us. About the wedding. I tell him I want him to stay out of my life.

SAM: So tell me.

KATIE: Stay out of my life.

(Pause)

SAM: O K. Keep going.

KATIE: And he turns and he asks questions.

SAM: Is Sam's cock bigger or smaller than mine?

KATIE: Um—

SAM: Answer.

KATIE: Smaller.

SAM: Does Sam make you cum like I do?

KATIE: No.

SAM: Not at all?

KATIE: *(Pause)* And I told him how we met and—

SAM: Do it.

KATIE: I met Sam because I was doing a show on office people. Taking pictures of office people. Businessmen, you know. And Sam was the only one who made me laugh. *(Pause)* I told him the rest, too, about how good I think you are. Just at making me feel better and healthy and he said—his answer is— "If you marry him, Kate, I will find you and every day I will knock on your front door."

SAM: I will knock on your front door.

KATIE: "And every day you will ignore me."

SAM: You will ignore me.

KATIE: "But, sooner or later, the front door will open."

SAM: The front door will open.

KATIE: "I will come into your house—"

SAM: I will come into your house.

KATIE: "I will put your camera in your hands and I will make you take pictures as I skin your husband alive."

SAM: I will skin him alive.

KATIE: He touched me.

(SAM *touches her face.*)

KATIE: And for the first time in my life, I told James good-bye. (*She stands.*) Goodbye. (*She tries to leave the apartment.*)

(SAM *leaps over the bed, slams the front door.*)

(KATIE *scurries into the kitchen.*)

(SAM *closes the blinds. The apartment is now even darker.*)

(SAM *slowly walks into the kitchen.*)

(*We hear* KATIE *scream. We hear the sounds of struggle.*)

(KATIE *starts to run out of the hallway before being yanked back into the kitchen.*)

(*Another struggle is heard.*)

(*Silence*)

(*Then,* SAM *comes crashing out of the kitchen, his hand over* KATIE's *mouth.*)

(SAM *throws her to the ground.*)

(*For a full minute, it gets more and more feral. Slapping. Clawing. This is really going to be a rape.*)

(KATIE *kicks* SAM. *Grabs the baseball bat*)

(SAM *picks up* KATIE's *camera. Disappears. He flashes it, blinding* KATIE.)

(*Every time he takes a picture,* SAM *disappears in the post-flash blackness. This happens three times. It should all feel like a horror film. You never know where* SAM *is going to pop-up next.*)

(*Finally,* SAM *mounts her on the ground, pulls down her pants.*)

KATIE: Do it.

(SAM *hesitates. Then pulls down her underwear. Hesitates again.*)

KATIE: Do it!

(SAM *takes off the Ken mask. Recoils and hits the bedside lamp, taking them out of the nightmare*)

KATIE: I did it for you.

(*For a long time,* KATIE *and* SAM *just sit there and catch their breath.*)

(*Their breathing finally slows.*)

(*After a long while,* SAM *picks up the Ken mask. They both stare at it.*)

(SAM *puts the Ken mask underneath the bed.*)

(*After a long pause, the lights fade.*)

END OF PLAY

www.ingramcontent.com/pod-product-compliance
Lightning Source LLC
Chambersburg PA
CBHW070030110426
42741CB00035B/2717